Contents

Welcome to Italy

The Republic of Italy, usually known simply as Italy, is located in southern Europe. It is a peninsula, or projection of land, stretching out into the Mediterranean Sea in the shape of a long boot with the island of Sicily at its toe.

Italy is slightly larger than the US state of Arizona and is more than three times the size of Great Britain. In addition to the Italian mainland, it includes several islands, among them Sicily and Sardinia, the two largest islands in the Mediterranean. Italy is known for its rich history, mild climate, fashionable clothes, art and distinctive food, based on pasta, tomatoes, olives and wine. Italian cheeses and ice cream are delicacies in many other countries, too.

Florence, an important historic city, is situated on the River Arno. ▼

Neighbours, states and regions

Italy is surrounded on three sides by sea. Its 2,000-km land boundary is shared with Vatican City and five countries – Austria, France, San Marino, Slovenia and Switzerland. San Marino and Vatican City, home to the Pope, are completely enclosed by Italy.

Italy was divided up into many small states until 1861. The states developed their own identities and customs, many of which survive to the present time, and give modern Italy its strong regional character, trade and tourism.

Country File
Italy

Ian Graham

FRANKLIN WATTS
LONDON•SYDNEY

Revised and updated 2006

Franklin Watts
338 Euston Road, London
NW1 3BH

Franklin Watts Australia,
Hachette Children's Books
Level 17/207 Kent Street
Sydney NSW 2000

COUNTRY FILE: ITALY produced for Franklin Watts by Bender
Richardson White, PO Box 266, Uxbridge, UK.
Editor: Lionel Bender
Designer and Page Make-up: Ben White
Picture Researcher: Cathy Stastny
Cover Make-up: Mike Pilley, Radius
Production: Kim Richardson

Graphics and Maps: Stefan Chabluk

Consultant: Dr Terry Jennings, a former teacher and
university lecturer. He is now a full-time writer of children's
geography and science books.

A CIP catalogue record for this book is available
from the British Library.

ISBN 0 7496 6641 2

Dewey Classification: 914.5

Printed in China

Picture Credits

Pages 1: Photo Disc Inc./Neil Beer. 3: Lionheart Books.
4: Robert Harding Photo Library/Ellen Rooney.
6: Lionheart Books. 8: Robert Harding/Mike Newton.
9: Robert Harding Photo Library. 10, 11: Robert Harding/
Mike Newton. 12–13: Robert Harding/Ruth Tomlinson.
14: Eye Ubiquitous/Bob Battersby. 15: Corbis Images/
Sygma/Alain Denize. 17 top: Eye Ubiquitous/Chris
Fairclough. 17 bottom: Robert Harding/B. Bott.
18: Corbis Images/Annie Griffiths. 19: Hutchison Library/
Julia Davey. 20: Lionheart Books. 21: Robert Harding/
Sheila Terry. 22, 23: Lionheart Books. 25: Robert
Harding/Simon Harris. 27, 28, 29: Lionheart Books.
30, 31: Photo Disc Inc./Neil Beer.

Cover Photo: PhotoDisc Inc./Neil Beer

The Author

Ian Graham is a full-time writer and
editor of non-fiction books. He has
written more than 100 books for
children.

Note to parents and teachers

Some of the websites listed in this book are in Italian but
most have the option to view in English. Every effort has
been made by the Publishers to ensure that the websites
in this book are suitable for children, that they are of the
highest educational value, and that they contain no
inappropriate or offensive material. However, because of
the nature of the Internet, it is impossible to guarantee
that the contents of these sites will not be altered. We
strongly advise that Internet access is supervised by a
responsible adult.

6°E   8°E   10°E   12°E   14°E   16°E   18°E

GERMANY

LIECHTENSTEIN

AUSTRIA

SWITZERLAND

46°N

SLOVENIA

Mont Blanc

Matterhorn

DOLOMITES

Bolzano

Lake
Como

Trento

Udine

Lake Garda

Lake
Maggiore

Trieste

CROATIA

Bergamo

Bassano

Piave

Milan

Vicenza

Venice

BOSNIA AND
HERZEGOVINA

Verona

Gulf
of
Venice

Turin

Oglio

44°N

Po

Ticino

Piacenza

Parma

FRANCE

Tanaro

Modena

Reno

Ravenna

Genova

Bologna

Rimini

Savona

Carrara

MONACO

Lucca

Florence

SAN
MARINO

Ancona

LIGURIAN
SEA

Pisa

Arno

Livorno

Arezzo

Siena

ADRIATIC SEA

Lake Trasimeno

Perugia

ITALY

Isle of Elba

Terni

Tiber

42°N

CORSICA

Pescara

ROME

Termoli

Foggia

Ofanto

Bari

Olbia

Naples

Mount Vesuvius

Brindisi

Alghero

Isle of Ischia

Potenza

Taranto

Tirso

Nuoro

TYRRHENIAN

Gulf
of
Taranto

Gallipoli

40°N

Oristano

SARDINIA

SEA

Cagliari

Crotone

Isle of San Pietro

IONIAN

MEDITERRANEAN SEA

Isle of Stromboli

38°N

SEA

Palermo

Messina

Reggio

Mount Etna

SICILY

Catania

Agrigento

Siracusa

Isle of Pantelleria

ALGERIA

TUNISIA

36°N

MALTA

Legend:
- Mountains
- Grassland and farming
- ☐ Capital
- △ Mountain peak
- ○ Major city
- Country boundary

0   200 Miles

0   200 Kilometres

N
W E
S

The Land

Italy is a very mountainous and hilly country. It is located where two great plates of the Earth's crust meet, which produces occasional volcanic eruptions and earthquakes.

There are two main mountain ranges on Italy's mainland – the Alps and the Apennines. The Alps run from east to west along the northern border and spill over into neighbouring countries. They contain some of Europe's highest mountains, including Monte Bianco (also known as Mont Blanc) and Monte Cervino (also known as the Matterhorn). The eastern end of the Alps includes the Dolomites. The Apennines run the length of the country.

Animals and Plants

Italy's varied landscape and mild climate supports a rich and varied wildlife.

Mammals:
Alpine rabbit, brown bear, chamois, ermine, fallow deer, fox, greater horseshoe bat, ibex, lynx, marmot, stoat, wild boar, wolf, monk seal.

Birds, Reptiles, Amphibians:
Black grouse, capercaillie, golden eagle, stork, flamingo, mountain partridge, alpine newt, alpine salamander, viper, garlic toad.

Plants:
Aleppo pine, ash, beech, carob, cypress, chestnut, green alder, heather, juniper, larch, lichen, maquis scrub, moss, Norway spruce, oak, oleander, olive, plane, Lombardy poplar, rhododendron, saxifrage, sedge, silver fir, willow.

The town of San Gimignano lies in the northern region of Tuscany, the landscape of which – rolling hills, cypress trees and small farms – features in many historic Italian paintings. ▶▶

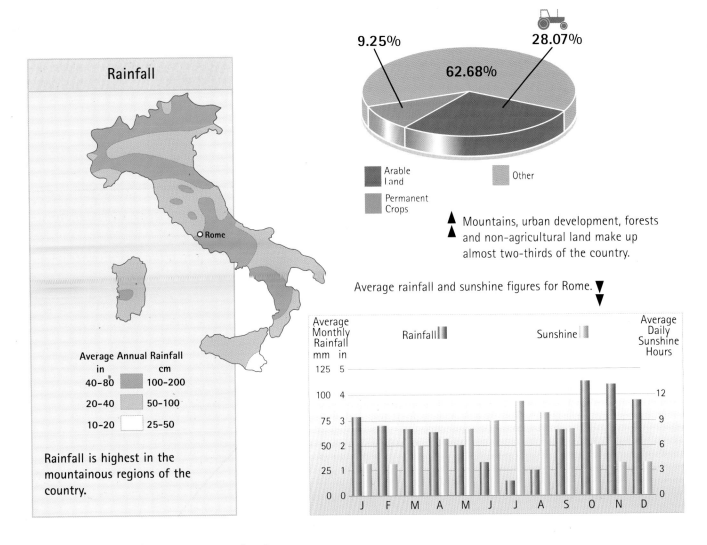

Rainfall

9.25% 28.07%

62.68%

- Arable land
- Other
- Permanent Crops

Mountains, urban development, forests and non-agricultural land make up almost two-thirds of the country.

Average rainfall and sunshine figures for Rome. ▼

Average Monthly Rainfall mm in

Rainfall ▮   Sunshine ▮

Average Daily Sunshine Hours

J F M A M J J A S O N D

Average Annual Rainfall

in		cm
40–80		100–200
20–40		50–100
10–20		25–50

Rainfall is highest in the mountainous regions of the country.

Volcanoes and ancient sea bed

Most of Italy's rivers rise in the Apennines. The longest is the Po. Some of Italy's lakes are flooded valleys that were carved out of the ground by glaciers. Others are flooded volcano craters. Italy has several active volcanoes, including Vesuvius, Etna and Stromboli. It was an eruption of Mount Vesuvius in AD79 that destroyed the ancient Roman cities of Pompeii and Herculaneum, burying them in ash.

The largest expanse of flat land in Italy is the Po Valley, the land surrounding the River Po. It was once part of the Adriatic Sea, the arm of the Mediterranean Sea that washes Italy's east coast. Over millions of years, the area gradually filled up with mud, sand and silt washed down from the mountains and became dry land.

Climate

Italy's climate is mild because most of its landmass is surrounded by warm Mediterranean waters. The hottest month is July and the coldest is January. The wettest is October and the driest July. The summers are generally warm and dry around the coasts and cooler higher up in the mountains. Winters are milder in the south than in the north.

The People

People have lived in the land of Italy for hundreds of thousands of years. Today, the population is about 58.1 million. Most live in the prosperous northern half of the country.

During Italy's long history, it has been invaded and settled by many different peoples from other parts of Europe and the Mediterranean. Their different cultures and influences have merged together to form the Italian people of today. The average age of the population is rising, as in many western countries, because the birth rate is falling. Italy was the first country in the world to have more people aged over 65 than under 15.

Italians buy cheese from a market stall in Siena, a town in the central region of Italy. Here, many people have ancestors from France, Germany and Switzerland. ▼

Language

The Italian language as we know it today has existed only since the country was unified. Until then, Italian was spoken differently in the regions. Some of the old dialects are still spoken at home in some places and within small communities. Near the northern borders, people often speak the language of the adjacent country.

A changing population

Italy has been a country of emigration since the beginning of the eighteenth century. Many people left because of poverty, especially in southern Italy. They also fled from the hardships of World War I and then the fascism that overtook Italy in the 1930s. Most settled in other European countries and North America.

Since the mid-1970s, immigration has increased as Italians have begun to return home in larger numbers and more people have also arrived from poorer countries such as Albania and Bosnia and Herzegovina.

Shoppers in Rome, where Italians speak with a distinct Mediterranean lilt.

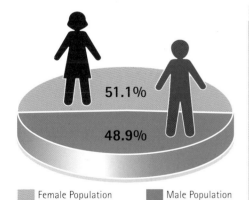

| 51.1% | |
| 48.9% | |

Female Population
29,683,963

Male Population
28,369,070

There are more women than men in the Italian population.

DATABASE

Ancient history

The earliest evidence of human settlement in Italy was found in Isernia, south-east of Rome, and dated to about 730,000 years ago. Another site near Verona is more than 400,000 years old. They are among the oldest human settlements in Europe. Remains of more recent prehistoric human settlements are found all over Italy.

Web Search ►►

► http://www.cia.gov/cia/
publications/factbook/
geos/it.html
The CIA World Factbook entry on Italy and its people, government and economy.

Urban and Rural Life

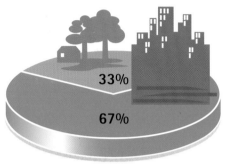

33%

67%

Percentage of Population
Living in Urban Areas

Percentage of Population
Living in Rural Areas

▲ About two-thirds of Italians live in towns and cities.

Venice

Venice is a unique city. It is built on 118 islands linked by bridges. Instead of roads and cars, its thoroughfares are canals and its traffic watercraft (see photo on the cover of the book). Its population of about 280,000 is overwhelmed by more than 10 million tourists every year.

Italians meet on a street in Bolzano, a town in Trentino-Alto Adige in the far north of the country. This mountainous region of Italy has many small towns and villages but no large cities. ▶▶

The difference between urban and rural life in Italy is not as dramatic as in many other countries. Many of Italy's towns and cities – most of which are in the north of the country – have retained much of their traditional charm and relaxed pace of life.

Italy's biggest cities, including Rome, the capital, have their share of modern buildings, but they are not the concrete and glass cityscapes found elsewhere in Europe. Industrialization came to Italy later than to other European countries, so the red-tiled roofs and cobbled piazzas of its old cities were not swept away in massive commercial and industrial redevelopments. One exception is Milan. Italy's economic power-house is more like London or Paris. Life in Milan is as fast and hectic as in any city anywhere.

◄◄ Farm workers gather olives on an olive grove in Puglia, a southern rural area that forms the 'heel' of Italy.

Population

Most Italians live in the flatter and more fertile north of the country.

○ Rome

Persons per	
square mile	square km
Less than 2.5	Less than 1
2.5–25	1–10
25–250	10–100
250–500	100–200
Over 500	over 200

The capital city

Rome is a special city. Once the most powerful city on Earth, its citizens still take great pride in being Romans. To live in Rome is to live surrounded by 2,000 years of history. The Colosseum, a great amphitheatre opened in AD80 and still a major landmark in Rome today, was the scene of savage combat between gladiators.

Rural life

In rural areas, people often follow a more traditional way of life. They are more likely to live in a close-knit family with perhaps three generations under the same roof. Their houses are typically grouped together in a village on a hilltop or among farmland. Each village has a small church and a marketplace. The peaceful surroundings, beautiful countryside, good food and mild weather of rural areas including Tuscany and Umbria make them favourite destinations for tourists seeking a relaxing break.

Web Search ►►

► http://www.guide2italy.net/umbria.htm
Website of the Umbria region.

► http://www.guide2italy.net/toscana.htm
Website of the Tuscany region.

11

Farming and Fishing

I taly's mountainous land makes much of the country unsuitable for farming. Despite this, Italy is almost self-sufficient in food.

The northern part of Italy concentrates mainly on the production of cereals, sugarbeet, soya bean, meat and dairy products. The southern part, with its milder climate, specializes more in fruit, vegetables, olive oil, wine and durum wheat. Wheat and rice are also grown in the fertile Po Valley. Most Italian farms are small and many of them have been owned and run by the same families for generations. Large quantities of citrus fruits, olives, olive oil, tomatoes and wine are exported. Italy is the world's leading producer of wine.

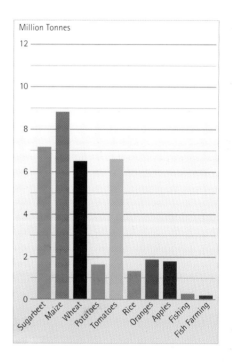

A comparison by weight of the annual production of major crops and the fishing industry in Italy. ▶▶

Farming Regions

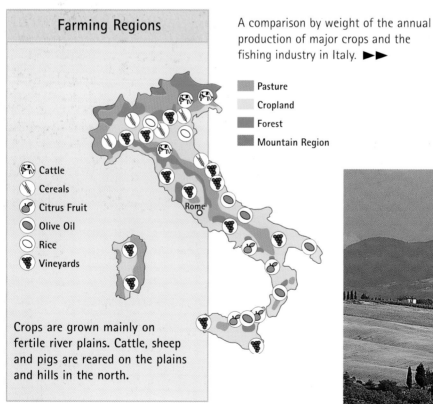

Pasture
Cropland
Forest
Mountain Region

🐄 Cattle
🌾 Cereals
🍊 Citrus Fruit
🫒 Olive Oil
◯ Rice
🍇 Vineyards

Rome

Crops are grown mainly on fertile river plains. Cattle, sheep and pigs are reared on the plains and hills in the north.

A view of wheatfields in Tuscany, after the harvest. Tuscany is a major agricultural region and central Italy's most important winemaking area. ▼

Commercial fishing

Italy has a fishing fleet of about 14,000 boats – some 15 per cent of the whole European Union fishing fleet of nearly 100,000 boats. The sea around Italy is divided into three areas – the west coast (Tyrrhenian Sea), the east coast (Adriatic Sea) and the islands (Sicily and Sardinia). The Adriatic fleet is the largest. The total fishing catch, including deep-sea trawling, fish farming and mussel and oyster beds, is more than half a million tonnes per year.

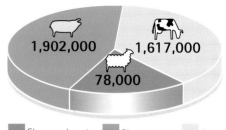

1,902,000   1,617,000

78,000

Sheep and goats   Pigs   Cattle

 The weight, in tonnes, of livestock reared in Italy for meat. Chickens are also reared for meat production

Parma specialities

Farms around the town of Parma in central Italy produce two of Italy's culinary delicacies – Parma ham and parmesan cheese. The hard cheese, which is aged for at least two years and is delicious grated over meals, is also important in the production of the ham. The delicately cured meat comes from pigs fattened on whey, a watery liquid left over from making the cheese.

 Small fishing boats at the dockside in Palermo, Sicily. These boats make short trips and small catches each day. Deep-sea trawlers spend many days at sea before returning to the docks to unload their huge catches.

 Web Search ►►

► http://www.embitaly.org.
uk/general/general_view
5.html
Information about agriculture in Italy, from the Italian embassy in London.

13

Resources and Industry

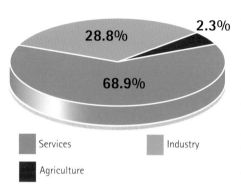

2.3%
28.8%
68.9%

- Services
- Industry
- Agriculture

▲ In recent decades, service industries such as finance, tourism and business have grown rapidly.

I taly's economy changed dramatically after the end of World War II in 1945. It rapidly developed from being based on agriculture into one of the world's largest industrial economies.

Italy has few natural resources. Most of the coal, petroleum and raw materials that it needs for energy, building and manufacturing have to be imported. Much of it is brought in by sea. Italy has one of the world's biggest merchant fleets. Natural gas is its most important mineral resource, yielding 18 billion cubic metres a year.

Italy's major industries are tourism, textiles, chemicals, vehicle manufacturing, shipbuilding, iron and steel production, food processing, textiles and electrical goods. Its manufacturers are mostly located in the northern part of the country. The government's attempts to develop and industrialize the south have met with mixed success.

Resources and Industry

- ✈ Aerospace
- 🚗 Car Manufacture
- $ Finance
- 🖥 Hi-Tech Industry
- ◉ Iron and Steel
- 👕 Textiles
- 👫 Tourism
- ◇ Salt
- ▢ Cement
- ▲ Pumice

Rome

Italy's major industries are concentrated in the north of the country.

▲ Italy is one of the world's biggest producers of marble used in building and sculpture. It is also a major producer of cement and steel.

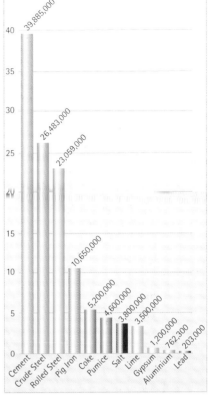

000,000 Tonnes

39,885,000
26,483,000
23,059,000
10,650,000
5,200,000
4,600,000
3,800,000
3,500,000
1,200,000
762,300
203,000

Cement · Crude Steel · Rolled Steel · Pig Iron · Coke · Pumice · Salt · Lime · Gypsum · Aluminium · Lead

▲ Annual industrial mineral production.

 Italy is one of the world's leading designers and manufacturers of high-performance car engines and bodies. Here, a prototype sports car is being assembled.

Designer clothes

Italian fashion is a very successful international business. The stylish designer clothing and accessories, made by fashion houses such as Armani, Versace, Gucci and Prada, are highly sought after around the world.

From small to global companies

Most of Italy's companies are small- or medium-sized, and many of them are family run. In the European Union, companies employ an average of 15 people. The average Italian company employs fewer than four people.

Although there are few large companies, some of them are so successful internationally that they have become household names all over the world. They include the car manufacturers Ferrari, Alfa Romeo and Fiat, the tyre manufacturer Pirelli, and the computer and business machine manufacturer Olivetti.

 Web Search ▶▶

▶ http://minerals.usgs.gov/ minerals/pubs/country/ 2001/itmyb01.pdf
Information about Italy's minerals industry from the US Geological Survey.

▶ http://minerals.usgs.gov/ minerals/pubs/country/ maps/94219.gif
A map of Italy's mineral resources from the US Geological Survey.

Transport

Travelling around Italy is fast and easy because of its extensive road and railway networks, ferries and air services. It also has a small network of canals.

Italy's cities are linked by express highways, called *autostradas*. Most of the autostradas are toll roads. Drivers must pay a fee to use them. Driving in Italy's cities can be difficult because of congestion and frequent traffic jams. Vehicles drive on the right side of the road.

Railways

After many years of neglect, Italian railways are going through a period of reform and modernization. Intercity trains are modern, comfortable and air-conditioned. Local and rural trains often use older rolling stock. Rome and Milan have their own underground railways, or Metros.

The two main long-distance railway lines are the *Tirrenica*, which runs from the French border to Sicily down the west coast, and the *Adriatica*, which runs from Austria and the former Yugoslavia down the east coast to Taranto. The *Pendolino* is a luxury service between Milan and Rome. It is expected to be extended to other parts of the country in future.

Air and sea

Most long-haul international air travellers arrive in Italy at either Rome's Leonardo da Vinci (Fiumicino) Airport or Milan's Malpensa Airport. European flights also arrive at Milan Linate, Naples, Pisa, Turin, Venice and some smaller airports. There are internal flights between most cities.

Italy's ports and offshore islands are served by a large fleet of ferries. Hydrofoils, which are boats that skim fast over the water, operate on some of the larger lakes and on some routes between the mainland and the islands.

Speed Limits

In towns, the speed limit for vehicles is 50km/h. On country roads, it is 100km/h on major roads, 90km/h on other roads. On autostradas, the limit is 110km/h for vehicles with engines smaller than 1100cc and 130km/h for larger vehicles.

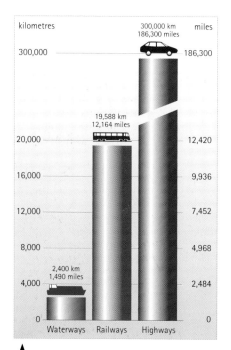

kilometres — miles

300,000	186,300
20,000	12,420
16,000	9,936
12,000	7,452
8,000	4,968
4,000	2,484
0	0

300,000 km / 186,300 miles
19,588 km / 12,164 miles
2,400 km / 1,490 miles

Waterways Railways Highways

▲ The Italian road network includes more than 6,000km of autostradas (motorways).

Major Airports

Major Ports

Motorways

Main Roads

Railways

The road, rail and air networks reach all parts of the mainland and major islands.

▲ Modern high-speed Eurocity trains bring passengers to the heart of Italy from many neighbouring countries, such as France, Spain and Germany.

◄◄The streets of cities such as Rome are often clogged with buses and cars. Many people use motorscooters to avoid being caught in traffic jams.

Web Search ►►

► http://www.fs-on-line.com
A website giving information about Italy's state railways.

► http://goeurope.about.com/od/rometransportation
Information on getting to Rome and around the capital city.

Education

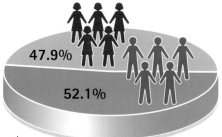

▲▲ In pre-primary (nursery) schools, there is a higher proportion of boys.

47.9%
52.1%

48.5%
51.5%

▲▲ There is a higher proportion of boys in primary schools, too.

DATABASE

Montessori Schools

The Italian doctor and educator, Maria Montessori (1870–1952) invented a new way of teaching children with obvious learning difficulties. Instead of traditional blackboard teaching, she encouraged children to use beads and bricks to help focus their attention on simple tasks and develop their manual skills. The system proved so successful that Montessori schools have been set up in many countries and continue to operate today.

Italy has a well educated population. The literacy rate has risen rapidly to about 98 per cent for both men and women. As recently as 1900, it was as low as 30 per cent in southern Italy, compared to more than 90 per cent in France and Germany at the same time.

Education is compulsory from the age of 6 to 15. It is free of charge at state schools but some parents send their children to private, fee-paying schools. The school day lasts from 8.30 a.m to 1.00 p.m. Monday to Saturday, or 8.30 a.m. to 4.30 p.m. with a one-hour lunch break, Monday to Friday.

Every year, up to 1.5 million children aged between 3 and 5 years attend pre-primary, or nursery, school. Just over one-quarter of these are private schools. Primary school begins at the age of six. Children learn a broad range of subjects, including maths, science, history, geography, languages, social studies, religious education, art, music and physical education.

Primary physical education includes play with all kinds of sports equipment. ▼

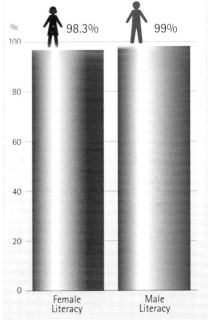

◄◄ Usually at the age of 11, children go from Primary to Secondary school. In some regions, between the ages of 8 and 12 children attend a Middle school before going on to secondary education.

98.3%   99%

▲ Literacy is slightly higher among men than women.

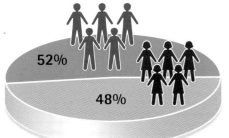

52%

48%

▲ In secondary schools, boys slightly outnumber girls.

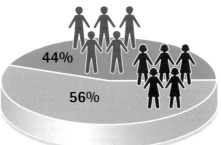

44%

56%

▲ Girls form a significantly higher proportion of university students.

Secondary and university education

At secondary school, children specialize in classical, scientific, technical or artistic studies. If they stay at secondary school for five years, they can take an exam for the *Diploma di Maturità* (Matriculation) in their chosen studies. Gaining this diploma grants admission to university to study for a degree. Students can then, if they wish, go on to study for a more specialized degree or diploma and then a doctorate (a PhD degree).

Web Search ►►

► http://unstats.un.org/ unsd/demographic/ products/socind/ illiteracy.htm

Information about illiteracy for many countries including Italy, from the United Nations Statistical Division.

Sport and Leisure

Italy is a nation of enthusiastic sports fans. Millions of Italians follow their favourite footballers, basketball players, motor-racing drivers and cyclists.

The most popular sport is football. Italian teams such as AC Milan, Inter Milan, Juventus, Lazio, Napoli and Roma attract enormous numbers of spectators for their matches. Italy's national team has won the World Cup three times, in 1934, 1938 and 1982. After football, basketball is the next favourite sport.

Italy has a long tradition of making beautiful cars that have enjoyed great success in international motor racing. Italians follow the fortunes of their racing teams and drivers very closely. Ferrari is one of the most successful teams in Formula 1 motor racing.

The modern Olympic stadium in Rome, where international athletics events are held and where both Lazio and Roma football clubs play. ▼
▼

Motor Racing

There are Formula 1 grand prix motor-racing circuits at Monza, near Milan, and at Imola in San Marino. The highspot of Italian motor racing is Maranello, near the town of Modena. This is the home and exhibition centre of the Ferrari company, where visitors can see some of its vintage and new racing cars.

Bocce

A form of bowls, called *bocce* or *boccia*, has been played in Italy for more than 2,000 years. Players take turns to roll balls as close as possible to a target ball. The winner is the player who gets the most balls the closest to the target. Italian emigrants took bocce to the USA, where there are now about a million players.

In summer, Italians and tourists flock to the beaches and holiday resorts along the coast, as here at the small town of Camogli in the Liguria region. ▼

Cycling and wintersports

Cycling is very popular, too. The *Giro d'Italia* (Tour of Italy), a three-week long cycle race, attracts huge crowds along the route to see the cyclists speed past.

Italy's snow-covered mountain slopes attract skiers and snowboarders from all over the world. The most popular wintersport resorts are Cortina d'Ampezzo, Courmayeur, Livigno and Sauze d'Oux.

Web Search ▶▶

▶ http://www.calcioitalia.8m.com/
A website full of news and information about Italian football.

Daily Life and Religion

Daily life in Italy revolves around the family, but times are changing and so are the traditional roles of men and women.

Daily life for women, especially in the major urban centres, has changed dramatically since the 1960s. Traditionally, men were the breadwinners and women looked after the home. Now, women no longer expect to spend their days at home. More women are staying in education to degree level and pursuing their own careers. Italian society is still male-dominated, but as more women work and study outside the home, Italian men have had to learn to share more of the home and family duties. Young Italians have readily accepted this cultural change.

The average lifespan of Italians is among the highest in the world. Women live an average of more than six years longer than men. ▼

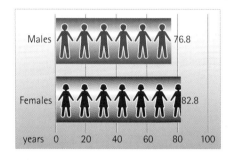

Males		76.8
Females		82.8

years 0 20 40 60 80 100

◄◄ The area of the 'Spanish Steps' in Rome, where some streets are closed off to traffic during the day so shoppers and tourists can walk freely. Pedestrianized areas are increasingly common in large Italian cities.

Food

Italian food has gained international popularity. Pizza, pasta dishes, rice-based risotto and speciality meats such as Parma ham and salami are eaten all over the world. Italian cheeses are very popular too – creamy ricotta made from sheep's milk, buffalo mozzarella made from buffalo milk, blue-veined gorgonzola and hard parmesan.

Opening hours

Opening hours for shops vary from region to region, but most are open from 9.30 a.m. to 1.00 p.m. and 3.30 p.m. to 8.00 p.m., Monday to Saturday. A long break for lunch, lasting one or two hours, is common. Larger stores stay open all day. Very few shops and stores open on Sundays.

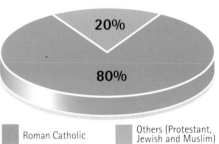

Roman Catholic	Others (Protestant, Jewish and Muslim)

▲ Four-fifths of Italians are Roman Catholic.

◄◄ Worshippers and tourists mingle outside the cathedral in Siena. Most cities and large towns have beautiful historic churches and cathedrals.

Religion

Vatican City, an independent state within Rome, is the capital of world Catholicism. Most of Italy's population is Roman Catholic. Church attendance throughout Italy has declined in recent years, but families still usually have their children christened even if they are not regular church-goers. People in rural areas attend church most regularly.

The Turin Shroud

In Turin, the *Duomo*, the cathedral, holds a remarkable piece of cloth. It was thought by many Christians to be the sheet that Jesus Christ was wrapped in after being crucified. However, in 1988, scientific analysis showed that this 'Turin Shroud' is no older than the twelfth century.

Web Search ►►

► http://www.vatican.va
The official Vatican website.

Arts and Media

Italy has one of the richest artistic and cultural heritages of any country. It has produced many of the world's greatest artists, sculptors and composers.

The Renaissance period, from around 1450 to 1700, when all forms of art blossomed across Europe, was centred on Italy. During this peroid, the *Mona Lisa*, probably the world's best known painting, was created by the Italian artist, scientist, engineer and inventor, Leonardo da Vinci. One of the most famous statues, David, was created by the sculptor Michelangelo. Galleries around the world display the works of these and many other Italian Renaissance artists, including Raphael, Bellini, Titian, Caravaggio, Tintoretto and Botticelli.

TV Broadcast Stations (total 358)

⬚ =10 Stations

Radio Broadcast Stations (total 4,709)

⬚ =100 Stations

▲ Italians have a wide choice of local, regional and national broadcasters as well as satellite channels.

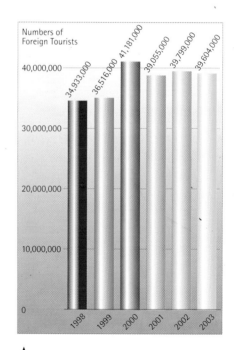

Numbers of Foreign Tourists

Year	Number
1998	34,933,000
1999	36,516,000
2000	41,181,000
2001	39,055,000
2002	39,799,000
2003	39,604,000

▲ Italy is one of the world's most popular tourist destinations. Visitors come from every continent, for beach holidays, sightseeing and winter sports.

Italians dress up for *Carnevale*, a major celebration that takes place in Venice each year to mark the beginning of the Christian festival of Lent. ▶▶

Opera and music

Italy is the home of opera. There are opera houses in all regions, including the world-famous La Scala in Milan. Musical works by Italian composers including Verdi, Puccini, Monteverdi, Rossini and Vivaldi are regularly performed all over the world. One of the best-known opera singers today is the Italian tenor, Luciano Pavarotti.

Cinema

Italian cinema is renowned for artistic and thought-provoking films. The best-known and most successful Italian film directors include Federico Fellini, Roberto Rossellini, Luchino Visconti, Pier Paulo Pasolini, Vittorio de Sica and Bernardo Bertolucci. In the 1960s, Sergio Leone made a number of popular western movies that became known as 'spaghetti westerns'.

The Media

Italian broadcasting was controlled by the government and heavily influenced by the church until the 1970s, when privately owned radio or television stations were allowed. Hundreds of new radio and television stations sprang up. A number of television channels, radio stations and newspapers are owned by one of Italy's most prominent politicians, Silvio Berlusconi, who was elected prime minister of Italy in 1994 and again in 2001. Most Italian newspapers are regional or focused on a particular city.

Overseas visitors

Italy is the fourth most popular tourist destination in the world after France, USA and Spain. Many visitors from northern Europe come by road, via tunnels through the Alps.

Web Search ▶▶

▶ http://www.operabase. com
A website full of information about opera, including Italian opera.

▶ http:/www.museionline.it
Information about museums in Italy.

Government

Italy has several different police forces. Most crimes are dealt with by the *Polizia*, the state police force. The *Carabinieri* is a military-style force that deals with a variety of crimes, including the activities of criminal organizations such as the Mafia. The *Vigili Urbani* deal with traffic and parking offences. There is also a force called the *Guardia di Finanza* that deals only with financial crimes such as fraud.

After World War II, Italy's monarchy was abolished and its constitution rewritten to ensure that it would be ruled from then on, not by a king, queen or dictator, but by a democratically elected government.

The Italian parliament is bicameral (it has two houses). The upper house is the Senate, with 315 senators. The lower house is the Chamber of Deputies, with 630 members. Senators and deputies are elected by the people for a period of up to five years. Politics in Italy is more turbulent than in most other European countries. Italy has had more than 50 different governments since it became a democratic republic in 1946.

Provinces and Territories

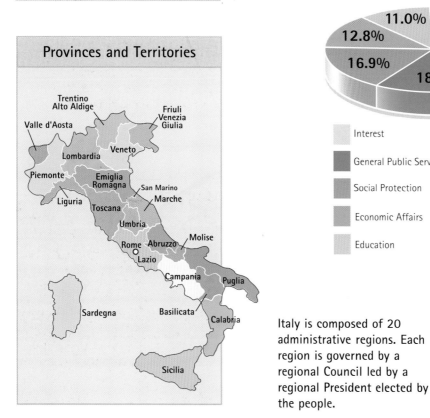

Italy is composed of 20 administrative regions. Each region is governed by a regional Council led by a regional President elected by the people.

4.8% 3.5% 2.8% 0.5% Housing and community amenities

0.5% Environmental protection

11.0% 7.6%

12.8%

16.9%

18.9% 20.7%

- Interest
- General Public Services
- Social Protection
- Economic Affairs
- Education
- Health
- Public Order and Safety
- Defence
- Recreation, Culture and Religion

▲ A high proportion of government spending goes on health, education and public services, giving Italians a high standard of living.

The President

The head of state, the president, is elected to a seven-year term by an Electoral College made up of the Senate, the Chamber of Deputies and representatives of regional councils. The president has a wide range of powers. He or she can call elections, dissolve parliament and appoint the prime minister. The president also leads the High Council of the Magistracy, which guarantees the independence of the law courts.

Government

The national government consists of the Council of Ministers led by the prime minister. At a more local level, there are 20 regions. Five of them (Sicily, Sardinia, Valle d'Aosta, Trentino Alto Adige and Friuli Venezia Giulia) have more autonomy than the others. Each region is divided into several provinces. At an even more local level, each province is divided into communes.

▲ A view overlooking most of Vatican City towards the historic centre of Rome. Vatican City was made an independent state in 1929. It has its own government and diplomats.

Web Search ►►

► http://www.italyemb.org/government.htm
Website of the Italian government.

► http://www.economist.com/countries/Italy
Information about Italy's politics and economics from The Economist magazine.

Place in the World

Chronology of Historical Events – up to 1800

1000 BC
The Etruscans begin living in Italy

700s BC to AD476
The Roman Empire. In AD330, the Empire was divided into East and West halves

AD485
Attila the Hun invades Italy

553
The Roman Empire is reunited by the Byzantine emperor, Justinian

800
Charlemagne, King of France, is crowned emperor of the Romans

814
Charlemagne dies. His son, Louis I, divides up the kingdom

962
The Holy Roman Empire begins under Otto the Great, King of Germany

1519
King Charles I of Spain becomes Emperor Charles V of the Holy Roman Empire

1700s
Spanish rule declines and Italy comes under Austrian rule

1796
Napoleon of France expels the Austrian rulers

Italy was once at the heart of an empire that stretched across most of Europe. The Roman Empire introduced more advanced roads, buildings, bridges and town planning, plus a common language (Latin) and legal system to the countries it conquered.

Today, Italy still plays an important role in European affairs. It is one of the founding members of the European Union (EU). More than half of its international trade is with other European countries, mainly Germany, France, Spain and The Netherlands. The government continues to promote the development of the poorer south of Italy to reduce unemployment, increase prosperity and narrow the gap with the wealthier north.

St Angelo's Castle in Rome was originally the burial place of Roman Emperor Hadrian. Then it became part of Vatican City. Now, Italy wants to claim it back as part of its history. ▶▶

International links

In addition to its membership of the European Union, Italy takes part in many international organizations including the United Nations (UN), UNESCO (the United Nations Educational, Scientific and Cultural Organization), the International Olympic Committee (IOC), the World Trade Organization and the World Health Organization (WHO).

A comparison of the value and major items of Italy's exports and imports. Income from tourism helps keep the country's trade profitable. ▶▶

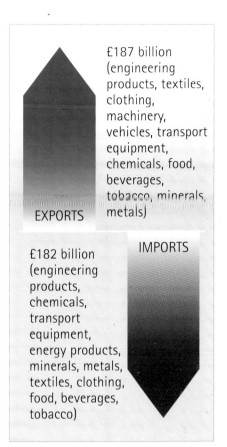

EXPORTS

£187 billion (engineering products, textiles, clothing, machinery, vehicles, transport equipment, chemicals, food, beverages, tobacco, minerals, metals)

IMPORTS

£182 billion (engineering products, chemicals, transport equipment, energy products, minerals, metals, textiles, clothing, food, beverages, tobacco)

DATABASE

Chronology of Historical Events – from 1800

1861
Italy's states are unified, forming modern Italy

1871
Rome becomes Italy's capital

1922
Benito Mussolini becomes Italy's dictatorial leader

1936
Italy forms an alliance with Nazi Germany

1940–41
Italy declares war on Britain, France, the USA and the USSR (Soviet Union)

1943
The Allies invade Italy. Mussolini is overthrown

1945
Mussolini is executed

1946
Italy becomes a republic

1970
Divorce is legalized

1978
Abortion is legalized

1984
Roman Catholicism ceases to be the state religion

2002
The Euro replaces the Lira as currency

◀◀ The annual children's international book fair in Bologna is the largest of its kind in the world.

29

Area:
301,278 sq km (including Sicily and Sardinia)

Population size:
58,103,033

Capital city:
Rome (population 2,775,000)

Other major cities:
Milan (pop. 1,369,000),
Naples (pop. 1,067,000),
Turin (pop. 963,000),
Palermo (pop. 699,000),
Genoa (pop. 679,000),
Bologna (pop. 404,000)

Longest river:
Po (650 km)

Biggest lakes:
Lake Garda (370 sq km)
Lake Maggiore (212 sq km)
Lake Como (146 sq km)

Highest mountain:
Monte Bianco/Mont Blanc
(4,807 m). The mountain straddles
the French-Italian border, with
the summit in France.
Highest mountain completely
within Italy: Gran Paradiso
(4,061 m)

Currency:
1 Euro = 100 cents

Flag:
Three equal vertical bands of green
(flagpole side), white and red

Languages:
Italian (official), German, French,
Rhaeto-Romanic, Sardinian, Slovene

Major resources:
Natural gas, pumice, feldspar,
aluminium, potash, asbestos

Major exports:
Engineering products, textiles,
clothing, footwear, machinery,
vehicles, transport equipment,
chemicals, food, beverages, tobacco,
minerals, metals

**National holidays and major
events:**
January 1: New Year's Day
January 6: Epiphany
Easter Monday: Pasquetta
April 25: Liberation Day
May 1: Labour Day
August 15: Assumption of the
 Blessed Virgin Mary
November 1: All Souls' Day
December 8: Immaculate
 Conception of the Blessed
 Virgin Mary
December 25: Christmas Day
December 26: St Stephen's Day

Religions:
Roman Catholic 83 per cent,
Others (including Protestant,
Jewish and Muslim) 17 per cent

Glossary

AGRICULTURE
Farming the land, including ploughing, planting, raising crops and raising animals.

BIRTH RATE
The number of babies born in a year compared to a set number of people, usually the number of babies born per 1,000 people in the population.

CLIMATE
The long-term weather in an area.

CULTURE
The beliefs, ideas, knowledge and customs of a group of people, or the group of people themselves.

ECONOMY
A country's finances, including imports, exports and government spending.

EMPIRE
A group of colonies ruled by a single country.

EXPORTS
Products, resources or goods sold to other countries.

GOVERNMENT
A group of people who manage a country, deciding on laws, raising taxes and organizing health, education, transport and other national systems and services.

GROSS DOMESTIC PRODUCT
The value of all goods and services produced by a nation in a year.

IMPORTS
Products, resources or goods brought into the country.

LITERACY
The ability to read and write.

LITERACY RATE
The percentage of the population who can read and write.

MANUFACTURING
Making large numbers of the same things by hand or, more commonly, by machine.

POPULATION
All the people who live in a city, country, region or other area.

POPULATION DENSITY
The average number of people living in each square kilometre of a city, country, region or other area.

REPUBLIC
An independent country whose head of state is an elected president.

RESOURCES
Materials that can be used to make goods or electricity, or to generate income for a country or region.

RURAL
Having the qualities of the countryside, with a low population density.

URBAN
Having the qualities of a city, with a high population density.

Index